NORTHWEST
Rainforest Pioneers

NARRATIVES & PHOTOGRAPHY

Claudia Harper

Frank Amato
PORTLAND

Acknowledgements

Clatsop County Historical Society and the Astor Library provided their archives of journals, diaries, and newspapers from the late 1800s and early 1900s. Many residents of Astoria and the Lewis and Clark River area, particularly those over 85 years old, shared their life stories and their families' life stories with me. Other residents freely lent me family photographs from three and four generations, especially Jim Russell, whose collection of old photographs was invaluable. Last, but not least, I want to acknowledge the tireless efforts of Marlena Montaine, technical assistant, who worked alongside me with the photos.

The North Pacific Coast is known for the beauty of its rivers, forests, and beaches; and Nature seems to work harder to keep a sharp rawness over the land. In the northwest corner of Oregon where the Columbia River meets the Pacific Ocean, natural forces set a particularly dramatic scene with huge evergreens, mountains of basalt rock, and rivers that wander then churn in threatening currents of water and sand bar.

Here at the mouth of this great river, settlers came soon after Lewis and Clark's expedition of 1805, and in six years the town of Astoria was founded. The promise of furs, and later, logging and salmon fishing, attracted immigrants from the Scandinavian countries as well as Greece, Italy, Germany, and China. These immigrants brought their trade, talents, and dreams to an area still untamed and at the mercy of rain, wind, and cold. Over the years, dairies and ranches covered the banks of sloughs edging the estuaries of Youngs River and Lewis and Clark River, subsidiary rivers of the Columbia. The people who ventured into this Youngs Bay area were isolated and self-reliant; the town of Astoria could only be accessed by muddy roads, eventually planked, and flat boats or skiffs to ferry them across the bay. Clusters of homes and barns eventually were built along the bay.

This book is a fictional narrative telling the story of one family—early settlers and the generations that came after them—through poetry and photographs. This book is also a narrative telling how the wind and rain, the rise and fall of tides, the soil, fire, and quick-changing sky affected this family. Some of them were determined, hard-working, and resourceful; others were unable to withstand the hardships and loneliness. But through time this family endured.

All inquiries should be addressed to:
Frank Amato Publications, Inc.
P.O. Box 82112, Portland, Oregon 97282
503.653.8108 • www.amatobooks.com

All photographs by the author unless otherwise noted.
The author was given rights free and clear by friends, family members, and collectors to use the photographs incorporated in this book
Book & Cover Design: Kathy Johnson

Printed in Hong Kong

Softbound ISBN: 1-57188-345-2   UPC: 0-81127-00179-8
1 3 5 7 9 10 8 6 4 2

Contents

Smoke

A thin gray wisp of fog weaves up over the hill
like her grandfather's cigarette smoke used to snake
from his gnarled yellow fingers as he sat out on the steps
at twilight next to the wooden slider
where her big brother rocked and rocked
and never talked even in daytime,
and Mama in her house-dress danced around the room
humming a tune and Papa stared right past her
from his torn leather chair in the corner of the parlor,
stared out to the woods where the moon always began.

It seemed the night hung there not ready to drop the dark
upon them, as if it were waiting, like maybe they were,
and she remembers scooting out on a tree branch
and scuttling up on the roof of the barn—
wanting to be somewhere high enough
to touch the first flashlight beam of moon
coming through thin trunks of cottonwoods,
and watching the shadow of the frayed-eared tomcat
that lived in the orchard as he crept in that waiting silence
through tall yellow grass to snatch the smoky moths
scattering the smoky light of the porch.

Family

Little Sister shapes her nails
in small arches of hope
that neat tidy
lady-thoughts will show,
while Grandma
points a nubbed, cut,
hang-nailed ragged finger
demanding manners,
for Great-Grandma
always washed her hands,
brushed her nails
white as the river pebbles
near the slough
where Great-Grandpa
gave up the planting
as the river flooded
thick with muck,
and Papa cleans
cow-clogged mud
from his nails with a jack knife
given by Uncle
who fished the river
pre-dawn til dusk
as proof
he really could pull himself up
by his bootstraps,
raise up Cousin,
beauty marred in rape,
her nails warped
like ripples in the sand
when the wind comes up

through the shuttered
sitting-room window
next to Grandpa,
who whittles at table
with gnarled-knuckled fingers
watching Auntie's
many-ringed hand
reach across
in a quick slap of
Elbows-off-the-table!
while Little Brother
pick pick picks at his plate
timed to the click
of clock boredom
and Big Brother
rocks and waits
til bread pudding time
with cinnamon cream and eggs
baked pridefully,
carried bowl-round
by Big Sister,
redclay-caked nails
marking savored tastes
from promised pots
and indifferent
to soap and scolding,
unlike Baby,
pink camellia-petaled nails
entangled in Mama's hair,
holding all
expectant family dreams.

Girlhood

Sun sliding down to make room for stars,
shadows slipping patterns like locust leaves
on curtains breezed by summer dusk—
evening sighs.

Mama embroidering rosettes
on Little Sister's pinafore,
the parlor cozy as sitting under
Grandma's quilt tucked and safe and warm.
And Mama gets that smile—the one Papa
said once almost knocked him to the floor—
and she hums and looks across to him.

She remembers when she was her daughter's age,
shimmying up Great-Grandpa's apple trees
each fall to reach the sunny ones on top,
remembers summers
gathering buckets of deep purple plums
to put up in winter jars,
how the sun was caught
in the boiling and pouring,
the stirring of sugar in pots,
and she remembers
crawling through banks of blackberries,
her face a mask of garnet seeds,
thorns sprouting on her thumb,
and the June evenings
when honeysuckle sweetened the stars.

Her sister and she would plan a tramp to the woods
and, after promises to be as careful as they could,
grab baskets and scamper across the open fields
to be first to find Fall's mushroom fairy ring,
then, nipping skirts up under tight knickers,
scurry up ferny hills into cool Spruce darkness
or collect wild iris and lady slippers in the Spring,
or wait in Summer thickness to hear warblers sing.

And, of course the rain, always there—
sometimes beating a soft reassuring drip
onto the garden cabbages and beans,
other times, lashing the wind,
so sheets of water passed up the road
like sails on a fleet of ships,
and her sister and she wrapped themselves
in Macintosh and high boots to tromp
and splosh hard through deep puddles
out to the barn where, rain or shine,
the cows still mooed for milking.

Mama turns to Papa in a tender shining,
says, *I hope our children will keep good memories*
to touch when evenings breathe deep.

Fences

The boy tilts the slats of shutters half-slant
to watch the moon
scooting along tops of pointing pine
before landing high on the edge of night.
Like a white bowl on shiny black oilcloth,
the crescent moon tips, pouring light
into long white lines through the slats,
flooding onto windowsill and door and quilt
til the room tingles in black and white stripes.

Throwing back shutters, he peers into the garden.
The moon shoots slivers of light
through winter alders lining the creekbed,
sketching a zebra fence of silver on black
around Mama's cabbage and rutabagas.

He remembers a December day
when only the black of fences
kept his way safe in blizzard snow,
when earth and sky were white on white
and his tears froze,
how Papa found him gripping the wooden stakes
even as he began to doze.

He remembers that last hot summer
when a back-beating sun hammered hard,
how Papa worked in dust,
kneeled and reached, lifted and twisted
to stake and wire those fences
until they were strong and solid
easing along the curves of green fields.

He thinks how Papa's tall shadow
stretches across the road
when the sun goes down under the ridge
to make room for the moon.
Papa, always straight and solid and sure—like the fence;
always holding to his word,
telling him *build for the hard times, boy.*

He can't imagine hard times, with Papa always there.
He closes the shutters, snuggles down into covers
dreams of stripes on the moon.

Butter

She squats on the three-legged stool,
string-hair stuck across brown eyes,
sweat rolling like little pearls
along fuzz hairs of white lanky arms.
On the porch scorching in heat,
she yanks the handle of a wooden churn
back and forth to quicken butter's turning
while the chirp of woman voices drifts
out the window and up to stacked clouds
crammed against blue arched sky,
and each breath of breeze repeats the stirring,
whipping dust-devils from a parched path.

She ponders how it happened the evening before,
when the boy down the road just sauntered up
and leaned on the porchstep rail.
He scuffed his boots, and drooped and stared,
finally muttered of fetching his Ma some butter
and glared at a splintered-board step,
then sputtered out a story of how he found his hound
while fishing when he took his skiff upriver,
his eyes kept lifting up and down real quick
as she listened between his words and summer's night air.

As the ambered porchlight flickered
around her unbrushed hair,
he stopped and grasped one straying curl, and blurted,
Your hair's so yellow—like honey or corn silk—
no, like butter...you know, real pretty, and ran off.
Now she wonders why he just tore down the path,
through the pasture, and forgot what he came for,
and his touching, the stirring turning her around, stays,
uneasy as tasting sour milk.

Moss

In the fog and drizzle, the distant winter trees
raise their mossy limbs in supplication for
more rain, but the dark clouds part, easing
a shard of sun through, striking the branches
bright and hard, lighting moss-grown roofs,
and all are transformed to jade—vivid green,
shadowed green, pale, precious, filigreed

like Mama's jeweled jade tree, delicate and small,
the one she kept beside her bed, brought over by
Great-Grandma from the old country she called
"Lost Dreams". Its leaves held mysteries,
earth's greens: jasper, emerald, serpentine,
and between, rested sea's blossoms: coral,
abalone shell, and pearl, all meshed in golden
strands like a net catching the world.

Brother was warned never to touch,
for discovery or even caress—much like his mother,
hard and mysterious, there on the porch brushing her hair
while the rain beads a curtain behind her, veiling
the maples up on the hill all still and naked
except for the moss, and the rain keeps a beat,
flailing the silence between them, her back stiff,
walking away from his hesitant, hungry need.

Clay

The rain whips down the hill in windy sheets
submerging the garden in puddles then pools
until all is soggy mud,
and she bends to gather it up,
brown and cool and grainy,
so she can squeeze it,
water dripping through her fingers,
til she holds a ball of dark earth in her palm.

She can breathe it, musky and pungent
with a promise of creation,
and memories come pelting
into her like raindrops—

of rolling clay into thin snakes,
setting one onto another to make a little bowl
while Mama shucked corn or opened peapods
and dropped green peas into a clay bowl
there on the wood porch by the warm kitchen
while they'd waited supper for Papa
in the twilight hour.

When he'd come up the porch
he'd yank off his boots all caked with clay
and tromp in, changing the kitchen
from hot pea soup and sweet cornbread
to damp sweat and wet earth,
and she'd rush for a hug
in his hard, lanky arms.

Later, he'd smoke and talk of spring planting,
how much soil might wash away from the rains,
how the marsh was flooding up
into the lower pasture and maybe he ought to
build higher up but what was a farmer to do—
all that damned clay on the hill.

Her big sister, clay underneath her fingernails,
would say it was a terrible waste,
and tramp up into the woods late at night,
put some clay in a hole of fire and ashes.
Whenever asked what she was doing,
she'd raise a bushy eyebrow, smile a secret way,
then answer, *Magic.*

Soon Mama would have a new bowl,
sketched with a bird wing on it,
or curled leaf, or coyote bones,
and whenever Mama said they looked real,
Sister always said,
Sure, their spirit is in the clay,
making them alive.

Now the rain falls and she pours tea
from a pot round and golden
with small dappled leaves
running around the base,
and a dragonfly on the edge of the spout
ready to rise from rocks in a shallow river bed—
reminding her of all she comes from.

Creek

In winter when rain is always ordinary,
the creek slides down corners of the east mountains
and winds a muddy brown like a snake sneaking through a forest, coils
down to pasture edge where it wanders like it won't pay no heed to
where it's going, twists and flexes and gets going a bit faster, so by the
time it passes the farm there's a hissing and gurgling going on, and it's
not so sneaky any more.

And Brother wasn't thinking when he got it in his head
to get sneaky, slipping out the window, slithering away quiet-like
from the porch lamplight to crawl down the muddy creek-bank
into the dark water—maybe remembering summer when it lay
shallow and cool for swimming easy under a sun that never gave up—
and lying there, he must have tried floating slow downstream
with no moon or stars to watch going by, just cold clouded sky
til somehow he drowned.

No one knew til next morning, when Mama, sick and tired
of calling him down for breakfast, finally went round to fetch him.
When they rolled a body out of the mud and stones, it lay puffed up like
an old catfish, white and floppy, and she was sure it couldn't be him.
Poor Mama just turned about the color of Brother and didn't even cry,

just tried to breathe while the men heaved the body up to the house,
carrying Mama's grief, and the neighbor women stayed,
to lay out Brother proper for burying, since it would be grieving hard for
Mama's final tending.

And after Brother lay under the bare maple tree—Mama's eyes tearless,
Papa's face furious—both stiff, looking down at that marker in the
ground like they were waiting for their son to get up and walk back to the
house with them, and after all the weeping and wailing had died down,
the neighbors came tromping inside for food and whiskey, and the room
filled with kind words
and remembrance
of how he never talked much but could call the crows so's they'd wing
down and walk along the fence, kind of curious, of how good a son he
was, seated there all day on the porch, never giving trouble, tipping back
and forth in Grandpa's rocker, grinning and nodding so agreeable and sweet.

Mama just left everyone speechifying and climbed the stairs,
and talk turned to other cares—-deer hunting and spring planting
and if the creek would soon flood.

Bouquet

She stands at the window
setting winter's last camellias in place,
a bouquet of softened pink,
and stares at the rain and wind blowing,
slowing down time.
Tops of trees wave and sway as if underwater
in a slow motion of changing currents,
swinging in rhythm
from height of trunk to budding branch
like a metronome set to moody March.

And the quiet of the parlor—
the stillness of her husband's leather chair abandoned
if it were not for his whittle knife
laying a gash of metallic light on the seat,
the solitude of Grandma's quilt
bunched up along the table for stitching,
the hush of her childhood doll sleeping
now thirty years since the giving
brings her to Time suspended
like an apple on a string
waiting bitter-sweet for one more bite.
And she remembers another bouquet,
how her two sons sent her flowers in the rain.

It seems her boys were just leaning over a narrow bridge—
the one Great-Grandpa built over the creek
to shortcut the pasture from the farmhouse—
and raindrops started to tapdance a staccato
and wind began to shuffle the rippled light,
wrinkling crinkles in the water.
Then a deluge broke out of the sky.
But no matter to the two of them,
leaning over the bridge to watch a rushing,
a hurtling of water over a stone dam
long ago laid up,
sounding a percussion of hiss and splash,
chasing and bubbling and spraying
like a miniature of the sixty-foot waterfall
back off the road a mile or so.

And as they followed twigs and dead leaves
leaping and floating that fast creek,
the idea came.
Her younger son spotted a flash of flower
tucked into tall wide leaves rising from the boggy ditch
its long neck craning an oval face to the sun,
a flower so yellow, waxy, and glowing

that Grandma called it the *Lantern Flower*,
bright enough to spot even in mud-brown water,
maybe with leaves wide enough to float
all the way down under the bridge
right to their Mama's garden.

So he stayed on the bridge, the older boy crossed
over, running upstream through the brush.
Grandpa had warned them
never to break off the leaves of this plant,
never even to touch it
because its other name, *Skunk Cabbage*,
meant something "powerful stinky."

But there ran his big brother
over blackberries and reeds lining the edge,
paying no heed to their thorns,
and tromped down into the river,
slushing in mud and weed,
plucked a bunch of leaves and flowers anyway.

He waded out deeper,
then squatted in the oozing mud
to gently set floating
golden ships of *skunk cabbage.*

The younger boy watched
the small fleet coming downstream
and pass under the bridge below him,
golden cups stumbling,
sinking, somehow rising
from their plunge over rocks.
They drifted to the creek bank,
docking at the foot of her garden.

And she, in the cloudburst
rushing to gather the last sheet from the clothesline,
scanned the bridge for her boys,

then scanned the creek level, just in time to see,
nestled in the reeds on the water's edge,
bright yellow flowers—a sunshine bouquet
sent in the rain especially for her.

At the window, now, she sighs
at Time's inevitable sadness,
her older son gone in a drowning winter-years before,
her younger, so long her little boy,
now on a far fishing boat.

She moves the camellia bouquet to the table,
caresses the curve of a dropped pink petal,
and gazes out
as the rain dwindles to drizzle,
leaving a heavy grayness
to veil her memories.

Night

Night comes brittle hard, and stars
flare glaring eyes down at the boy
hunkered in hay next to his hound dog
dead now from gunshot after galloping
amok through the neighbor's hens.
Papa said *No bawling for boys,*
just bury it and call it a lesson—and
next time keep it tied; but try as he can,
somehow the grieving comes to be.

The boy stares out through the open
barn door to the far woodside hill
where bare fingers of trees hold up
a heavy nightsky, watches dark clouds
come cluttering in to hide the accusing
stars, clouds piled like black bales of hay
across a midnight pasture, watches
until a storm cracks the black open
and the night rains black tears.

Welcome

Grandma sits by the window
as the wind tosses the trees,
and daffodils bend and tatter
in the rough hands of a storm
doing its best to scatter Spring,
just as that first day she arrived
after saying good-by to girlhood
and welcoming the world of marriage.

~

Two days on the steamer up the coast,
a bride at fifteen brings her dowry—
heart, deep Norwegian woods; eyes, icy fjords,
fishing and farming running to the bone,
a true daughter of the sea—
so the weather-boiled waves and tides,
the rugged raw county she breathes
when she arrives at the rivertown
feel like the first leg of a journey...home.

Clutching the bonnet tight to her hair,
she hires a buggy to drive there past the point,
and in the bluster of March's cold rain
takes a boat fording the bay, trying not to hear
the rising beat of her anticipation
as she nears her tall young husband.
Holding a defiant umbrella in one hand
and lifting her skirts above her ankle with the other
to deter licks of little waves about her feet,
she steps ashore into his eager arms.

The long road, more mud and stones than road,
jostles and jerks the cart winding round open pasture,
where placid sheep and cows graze, indifferent to the weather,
two matched chestnuts—her new husband's pride—
fly to get back to the farm as dark thunder clouds rumble,
clustered overhead, so that as the storm explodes,
scattering apple trees' white blossoms like snow flurries,
the cart slows to a shivering halt, and he whisks her up,
lifts his bride over the threshold...and into her new life.

~

Now the wind
sweeps the garden
clean of uprooted weeds.
Grandma sighs,
and Spring slides
across the window
for one more year of memories.

Hail

The sun sat all day on the horizon,
a crushed peach squeezed between
gray strings of clouds/slipping past
like dark haunted ships, while
the battered gray bay churned to constant
wind, gripping tops of cedar and
and turning whipped branches of hemlocks
into feathered wings of great green birds
perched on the thin line of hill and sky.

Now, on tiptoes, the child peers from the sheer
lace curtains out to the day, colored cold
pink-gray, like a treasured agate marble.
She pretends the starting raindrops wiggle
transparent inchworms, crawling down the pane
to measure the sky's twirling image.
So when night finally turns,
shutting the day down dark and starless,
she gasps in delight at a sudden tap-tap-tap
of hailstones rapping the porch roof, bouncing
on the steps before settling in the vegetable
garden to seed the pleated cabbages in white.

Mama slips behind her, so their gaze stays
paired in bright reflection by the window,
and she strokes the girl's curled brown hair,
remembering her own first day of hail, when clouds
seemed to break into pieces and she rushed from
the schoolhouse, lifting her long skirts up
away from mud sucking her boots, and waded puddles
pricked by bouncing white balls, then caught
all the bits of sky in her lunch bucket.

The little girl opens the door and scoops up
a handful of white beads, raising them between
her teeth, as the melting ice begins to slide through
her small fingers, and laughs, *I'm biting the sky!*
Mama smiles and looks into the child's dark eyes
mirroring her own deep brown, and recognizes the joy
in the passing of pleasures one generation to the next.

Mustache

On the first of August the boy's sky grows wings of clouds,
tapered, stretching like pelican feathers.
But as the sun grows warmer,
wings change to mustaches, thin at either end,
wide and gray like Uncle's mustache.

Uncle—the one who is a logger and always tells tales
til the boy isn't sure what's true and what isn't.
Uncle holds up his white finger,
numb from gripping the saw,
and tells of the screaming, rasping shrieks
he hears when wood fights against saw,
loudness boring into his head all those wood-cutting years.
The boy thinks that must be reason Uncle says *What? What?*
when he tries to tell him something.

Uncle tells of walking the trees with spurs on his calks—
like a rodeo cowboy, the boy thinks;
tells of a barber chair top of tree,
swinging back, sending a climber
flying, dropping, dying.
If the boy waits quietly, Uncle tells again
the story of his little cousin a few years back
just watching his Pa working the water's edge,
logs sliding down the skid tracks,
rolling together into the slough.
And suddenlike, how the logs flew down,
jamming, pushing up and over one another
like hungry hounds, and swallowed up his little cousin—
gone before you blinked.
Uncle pulls and twists his mustache after that tale.
The boy thinks he jerks his mustache pretty hard
'cause Uncle's eyes always water.

Evening, when the sky turns peach jam
and the spruce on the hill
look like they're ready to taste it,
Papa and Uncle sit on the porch;
talking of cows and maybe putting up a new barn.
Papa's hands whittle a little flute
Uncle's hands finger his mustache,
and the boy wonders at the flute's song,
wonders if his face would ever like a mustache.

Morning

At dawn he sets out for the lake.
He anticipates the fish, the quiet.

And he finds himself stepping
silent to its edge,
as if it were still sleeping.
In the beginnings of light,
the water lies dark,
hinting of murky depths,
except for thin lines of light
wavering like spinning snakes
from the rising sun's pink fingers
reaching through mossy trees.
Light changes with each breath,
so that in just a few moments,
pieces of the surface turn silver,
and shimmer in beginning-blue
like small pools rising
from a dark green pond.
When the sun manages to climb
up the firs and cedars,
shoots of blinding light
pierce the calm waters
and spotlight a dance
of yellow trees in the farside forest.

Crows call a raucous refrain
repeated from tree to tree,
and gulls squawk and circle
before escaping to the sea,
leaving a nearby squirrel
to chatter back.

The air warms,
and insects flick and flirt
with airborne seeds
drifting above the water.
A fall breeze teases the lake
so it shivers a second,
then lies still.

Suddenly the surface,
clean and smooth as paper,
pops silver holes;
small punctuation marks
–commas and exclamations —
hop, skip, twist
as small fish leap,
delighting in an early breakfast.

He throws his line out.
Morning is awake.

Fields

At the base of the wooded hill, fields of furrowed earth
rolled in chocolate waves rising in crests, troughs dipping low
ready for the seeding.
Great-Grandpa treads the rows, the boy trailing,
and the sky flocked with crows and promises of rain.

Great-Grandpa bent, his hard, gnarled hand scooped a sift of soil,
and he pressed it to his veined nose, taking a long sniff,
then rubbed the soft darkness slipping through his fingers
back to the ground
My boy, you know, it's the feel of it, the smell,
tells you it's ready for growing.

He swung the wooden gate to the long muddy road
leading to a clumped pasture, lumped in mole hillocks
and pockets of bog from the black cow's wanderings.
As they ambled the edge of the meandered river
the boy matched strides alongside Great-Grandpa.
White bones of alder still hadn't sprouted Spring
and barren sticks of bracken and blackberry hid the path
back of the farm house. They tromped along, silent,
with only the scream of a hawk high above.

Great-Grandpa spoke again, clearing his throat with a loud hack,
and the boy slowed his pace in expectation of a story.
With hoarse, husky words Great-Grandpa told of another field
in the old country, a field once thick with grain and crops,
then swept clean of anything green, as famine galloped
through his village to the small settlement of farms down the road,
pillage and kill its purpose til all was desolation complete.
And the land lay bleak and dry, empty of all but furrows rising
of fresh-dug graves, the good people rolled into them like seed sacks,
no one saved. That's when the family braved the sea for a new country.

The boy tried to see their own farm, a place he'd known forever,
the greening pasture, the tufted fields, the wide barn and warm home
suddenly gone, ...but it was too hard.
Great-Grandpa reached out his hand to grasp his shoulder
When you're older, boy,
give this land respect and sweat
and it will give you back a man's pride.
Hold on to the land.

Fire

Summer caught fire/
fir and spruce, hemlock and pine
writhing in burnt agony,
gasping one last breath into smoky skies.
Grandma stands on the back stoop,
hands gripping the porch rails,
mouth grim, face stoic,
watching.

She remembers—too vividly—
those first days of living on the land,
fresh from city life, no ranch girl she,
the shudder of fear
when her new husband proudly drove her
into a forest of trees
and called it home.

And he worked day and night,
tenacious, determined,
cleared vine-maple underbrush,
cut logs, split shakes to build a cabin for her.
Once done, he turned his will
onto the dense wall of trees—
auger boring into thick hides of giants
while she kept a fire going,
carrying coals to place in holes,
pressing bellows to start a blaze
inside the belly of each tree.
So many trees to burn,
so many fires surrounding her in a circle of heat,
intense, constant, blackening the air,
burning her skin til she could stay no longer.

With a promise to return, she hitched the horse,
wide-eyed, snorting fear—fled
down the puncheon road,
hoofs and wooden wheels bouncing spruce planks,
rushing to safety of neighbors
five miles away.

Evening brought a roiling:
swelling clouds and thunder-rain.
Fires drowned that night.
On her return, there the cabin squatted,
hunched and beaten,
the land crusted by black bodies of trees.

From that clearing their ranch sprouted—
apple orchards, gardens of summer dahlias,
carrots and cucumber, potatoes and beets,
Holstein butter and cream, milk and cheese
and a family—four sons and a daughter—
thrived on hard work and love.

Now Grandma smiles,
nods at incoming sheets of rain,
clouds blown by wind upriver,
sighs in the recognition of comings and goings—
the tides, the forests,
the fires, the cooling rain.

Cow

He wakes to wet silence,
fog filling every bird song, every log fell,
and he strolls the cloud around his feet
on the path down to the pasture.
Damp drops prickle his face
and his boots pull heavy sucking in bogged mud.
In the mist-hush of his solitary walk
he feels a jarring in each step,
the tingle of body meeting earth,
and he holds the moment
to breathe deep a contentment of heart.
Then from the thickness of fog
comes a plaintive bawling—
a calf crying for its mother,
and he can't help but smile
recalling the storm morning nigh sixty years ago
when Papa kicked open the back door
and stomped into the warm kitchen
with a newborn calf in his arms.
Here, she's yours, better feed her.

He remembers it was bottles and bottles
and lots of sweet words and petting,
til the calf felt more than at home,
following him from kitchen to bedroom to parlor
over the next month or so.

Mama told him the calf bawled
off and on when school came around
so he dreaded that two-month-old time
when the calf would join other heifers.
That day he'll never forget—
led down to the pasture, summer grass high and rich,
that calf just leaned against the fence and bawled some more.

But she grew big and strong with eyes like liquid earth,
and when Papa brought the cows up the road,
his cow always managed to slip away—
just mozied up to an open window
and gazed in, a nostalgic look on her face,
perhaps she, too, remembering her past,
those calf-young years,
hoped for a moment's pet, a tender rub to her forehead,
a gentle reassurance that, old as she was, she was still loved.

NORTHWEST
Rainforest Pioneers

River

He sets off before dawn, lifts the light boat
upon his rounded shoulders, skein and line and pole
all intricate spider webs caught in the drifting starlight.

He pads barefoot through slick mud and weeds
down to the river's edge where the water cuts deep
between mountains curved into the palm of night.

He pushes off, boat sliding from brushed earth to liquid silver
as easy as a sigh, and from the dim escarpment
come whispers in the damp air, scents of loam and pine.

He drifts and slips silent, steady in the gliding,
only the dip and drip of paddle in and out of water
announce the shift of dawn crowning the sky.

Brown-tapered rushes bow to his soundless procession
along the flowing river, and their thin delineation
is repeated in the distant undulation of wings in flight.

The river's swift current courses the floating boat
so that he is free to lean to the skein, play out his line,
slicing the sheen of water like a ripped seam on a silver kite.

The boat shivers in the slivers of water radiating pink
from the fingers of morning, and he stands, pole in hand,
head bent to the submerged world, a patient stork awaiting fish to bite.

Today

The alders lean just past the gate like thin
exhausted farmers and the bogged pasture
is pocked with black cows still as old stones.
She glances at the wintering plants abandoned
along the porch and wonders if today
can be any different from yesterday
with winter set and her husband gone til spring—
and she is too far from evening.

Late morning brings no freshness and
clouds hang like gray wet blankets
heavy, ominous with threat to drop
and break something; so she dismisses
the wash and brings in the hound, just as
hail falls like small white marbles, bouncing
on the shed roof, rolling and piling up on
the dark barren soil until all is buried
in white—and somehow she is relieved.

By afternoon, turbulent clouds surge along
the nearby river and she wraps herself up
to tromp outside and barn the animals,
their steamy fur, their acquiescence
familiar and reassuring; so when she returns
to the warmth of the kitchen, she prepares soup,
dwells on the chopping and slicing,
the orange of carrots, the green of celery,
the waver of bay leaf and oregano stirred and simmered
all combining to offer up comfort.

There are so many yesterdays she refuses to let in
as they knock and push one another,
and when she stokes the fire,
the memory of her small son's dimpled hand
bursts her mind—a moment of delightful wholeness
too quickly followed by a tearing, ripped gash inside her
as she sees again the small granite cross
under last spring's dogwood.

She sighs and stirs her soup,
waits for evening to come in,
bringing shadows to enclose her,
sleep to embrace her
until another tomorrow.

NORTHWEST
Rainforest Pioneers

Grasses

The sky is a blue pond
with gray-white lotus-flowers
floating slowly along its surface,
and the curves of gray/white gulls
emerge and dissolve in their drifting.

The boy and his sister cut through the garden,
their goat tromping between them,
and they tramp past the last house,
cross a wooden bridge, and follow the dirt path,
ignoring the occasional blackberry vine
reaching out to catch their attention.

The sister leans
into a thicket of bright scotch broom,
breaking a branch of its yellow-beaked buds
to clear the way for her little brother,
then leads him to an abandoned apple orchard—
gnarled trees fluttering small white flag blossoms,
surrounded by a silvered field of grass.

Both children lie down,
pillowed in grass blown to the whims of wind.
Eyes closed, they surrender to sun and sky,
scent and sound seep into their noses, their ears—
the grasses hiss wind's secrets into their very skin.
The sky suddenly darkens in black shadow,
cold slips between earth's warmth
and the quivering air around them.

Tall as the boy, the thin blades rise
in bone-white and emerald-green stalks,
and buff tufts of seeds top the waving leaves
twisting and turning in the lifting breeze
like small beacons to the sky's shifting light.
Wind ripples the field in wavering rows
as if it were part of the nearby river.

The goat wanders through the field,
its boney haunches seem to drift
along the surface of grassy waves.

When small beads of hail
bounce on their heads and shoulders,
they take hands and laugh
in a wild run through a river of grass,
leaping, bounding, spinning in one place
until the bent grass cushions
like a hidden nest for wild birds,
and they sink down onto the bed of icy grass
to watch the white-capped river.

The wind sweeps off the water,
throws the last bits of hail
at the shivering apple blossoms
until they let go, rise, swirl
like white birds taking flight,
then spin and sink
in a slow float
down onto the grass around them,
offering the children one last white whisper.

Claudia Harper

Neighbor

Underneath the shallow slosh
of wooden bucket-water,
with a wood-slipped comb
in her long yellow hair
she shimmers lemon in soapfroth.

Across the musky summer-grass
beyond the bluejay's warning cry,
beside his shaggy one-eared mule,
he gazes hard at her bent form.

Down his beaten mind,
past the broken glass of boyhood,
past tobacco Papa, vacant Mama,
he stirs that long-ago hunger up

~

of a steamy washday,
he in sixteen-year-old heat,
another girl, ebony-haired,
leaning over a oilcloth table
arms and breasts bare
in her solitude,
unaware of his coming.
He with sucked-in breath
steps to the girl,
her dark-deer eyes widening
when he reaches out,
grasping that giving flesh
silky as a pony's muzzle,
warm as a cow's teat,
and she, her cries and tears
like a summer storm
soon silent in the numbness.

~

Now he stalks a path to her,
a dry-dust appetite rising,
ready for the touch, the taste of her,
the dawn of fear in her—
she who combs her yellow hair
innocent in sunshine.

Clearcut

Out in the grazing pasture,
the old Morgan,
once a blazing chestnut of rush and gallop,
now horse-easy in the chomping and walking,
seemed a bit frisky,
and followed the boy with attentive eyes
as he strolled along the fence.

And the spring day floated a lightness
and beckoned the boy—
yellow field daisies spotting the pasture,
quick strokes of clouds
dashing along the flat slate sky—
and somehow the horse
looked so contented and willing.

Before the boy knew what he was doing,
he'd climbed the fence, straddled the Morgan.
The horse looked downright pleased
as they trotted to the gate
and the boy leaned over to unlatch it.

Well, that horse knew freedom when he saw it,
because he took off
out to the road and up the hill,
with the boy hanging on to the horse's neck,
heels digging deep,
just like he was racing Spring itself.

The path thickened going up into the woods,
heaving of the galloping horse and excited boy
beat a rhythm in the silence around them.
Ascending the hill cresting the next ridge
the horse slowed to a walk, then stopped.

Ahead was nothing but felled trees
dry and flaking like smoked fish,
the ground around, a burial site for once giants.
As far as eyes could see was not the green
of Douglas fir and white pine
but brown and rust-red of mud and stump,
shattered, torn trees: yew and birch and maple,
all discarded like forgotten Lincoln logs
of some negligent child.

The horse stepped gingerly onto uneven ground,
and, as the boy neared the clearcut,
he found Sitka spruce and cedar torn from roots,
splintered, sliced, flayed, split
as if ripped limb from limb in the mayhem of
a mad surgeon.

He couldn't name it—the sadness, the shock.
He could only turn the horse around
and descend the hill slowly,
pondering a darkness coming on him,
the sudden heaviness of Spring.

Gray

A thin peninsula of graying clouds
slips slowly across the sky
softly caught on the drift of wind
going north over the bay,
and the shift of grays,
muted blues and purple,
changes in the light
like the feathers of a pair of doves
her grandmother used to keep,

their gentle persistent coo
waking her each summer morning
so she could watch the sunlight
finger its way to her arms and face
until the hovering scents
of bacon and eggs,
and buttermilk pancakes
enticed her to hop into clothes
and scamper downstairs
to be the first served,
only to find Grandpa
way ahead of her,
and Grandma
pouring his second cup of coffee,
doling out four more bacon strips,
fetching his favorite marionberry jam,
nodding and circling him—
attentive as one gray dove to the other
in feathered-soft devotion.

Later, Grandma sewed
her first silk dress,
not blue or red, but gray,
and when slipped over her head
it shimmered in translucence
like a dove's breast in the sun,
so she felt one with the silvered sky
that first night she went out and danced.

Bull

It's dusk, and light glows beyond the pasture.
Up on the hills each bush and tree threads silver.
Papa and Uncle, after the evening meal,
a cordial, down-right friendly meal,
sit out on the dimming porch,
Papa in his rocker and Uncle whittling a bird,
both looking out at the sky.

They begin one of those talks—
the kind that always end in shouts and stomping—
usually about the cost of cattle or fish or timber—
and Papa always gets up first, muttering about Uncle
He's so bull-headed—
charges in without a thought and never backs down.
Uncle always stamps off, mumbling about Papa
He don't know the difference between night and day
and takes 'im that long to make up his mind.
Mama comes out about then, says good-night
so everything kind of goes back to quiet.

Now morning, with a wet white sky you could
spoon up like pudding,

they sit nice as you please,
enjoying Mama's pancakes,
talking about moving the heifers
up to the pasture nearer the barn
and how Uncle's prize bull might win
again at the County Faire.

Off they go in the old truck,
jackets buttoned for a damp autumn day.
The boy traipses after Mama,
doing his chores in the house and up in the barn,
and time ticks not so quick.

By noontime the drizzle and mist are giving in,
tired of fighting sun's persistent nudge to move on,
and Papa crunches the gravel path to the back. After
splattering his sweaty face in the tub,
he steps through the kitchen door
roaring about addled-brained heifers.
Over hot soup and fritters, he kind of sighs
how heifers sure are reluctant to change pastures,
and when he pushed back his chair,

mumbles how Uncle's bull in the next field
makes quite a racket since those heifers moved out.

Mama smiles and mentions the bull Grandpa had,
the one Grampa trained to pull a sled,
and how neighbors shook their heads,
seeing that load of turnips and beets
tipped high and heavy,
and the bull ploughing along easy as you please.
Papa chuckles and says
that old man always could tell a good story,
and thanks Mama for a fine lunch.

Then hunching up his shoulders to slip on his coat,
he tramps out to his truck, calls the boy to join him
figuring they might as well check on that noisy bull.
Of course, the boy jumps at the chance
and scrunches up front,
Soon both bounce along, Papa letting the boy steer.
Sure enough, when they got near,
past the chestnut tree Great-Grampa planted 1883,
you can hear the bull bellowing.
A heifer—really a pretty little Holstein—
stands looking kind of lost,
alone in the field fenced off from the prize bull.

Now, I thought your Uncle took all them in—
how'd she get left behind? Papa asks
as he reaches under the seat to find some rope,
then straddles the fence and walks towards her,
whispering and humming so she'd not bolt.
She comes quiet-like,
and as Papa ties her to the back of the truck
the bull roars out a ponderous complaint,
then, glowering,
barrels headlong towards the fence.

Hope that fence holds him Papa says under his breath
as he marches back to get in the truck.
The boy turns just in time to see the bull
thunder forward and lift his huge body up—
right over the fence—to land on the road!
He jumped the fence! Papa gasps,
stashing the boy under the truck
as the bull charges straight,
snorting something furious.
Horns lowered, snot dripping,
he strikes the side of the truck
like it was another bull and a fight was in order.

There they stand—heifer bawling, boy quaking,
Papa swearing and the bull shaking its head,
stunned but determined.

I never did hear of a bull doing such a thing!
declares Papa,
and grabs an old broom—
starts swinging and calling,
the bull stabs at the truck
and keeps snorting and pawing.
With all this clamor and pandemonium,
the neighbors come for a closer look,
and after much debate,
take a couple of roped heifers
down into the field as decoys, and open the gate.
To everyone's relief,
the bull decides to meander on back to get acquainted.

The boy crawls into the front seat,
but, as the wounded truck grinds its gears
to bring the little Holstein roadside up to the barn,
he can still see that flying vision:
foam around the mouth, fierce glare in the eyes,
ripples of quivering muscle.
Boy! After all that,
Uncle's not so bull-headed, huh Papa?

Geese

Trekking in tall yellow grasses
bent to mist and winter wind,
she catches a call, distant,
dimmed in heavy cloud,
and recognizing the familiar,
looks up expectant, but nothing
punctuates the whiteness above.

As the cry resonates again
in the wind, a wide-arrowed V
of wild geese crosses the bay
skimming the ceilinged sky,
piercing the weather
with dauntless determination,

so like Great-Grandpa's
unfaltering purpose—
even in his last days,
his jutting chin led him
stubborn and sure,
his large hook nose
still pointing the way,
there on the map
of his ninety-year face.

For he had kept the promise,
his purpose unwavering:
to go northwest
to harness the land,
to raise up a farm
for Grandpa and later, Papa—
the sweat on his shirts,
the cracks in his hands
told his story.

And she recalls Papa tromping
winter mornings deep in soggy
grass, his long stride speeding
her ten-year-old legs double time,
his rough, big hands enclosing her
cold fingers. They jump furrows,
climb fences, watch crows circle
and caw past the barn
before settling in naked sticks
of alder lining the edge of woods.

They step out into the field
where Papa stops, stoops over,
and after fingering the mud,
hands her his discovery—
a black, jagged arrowhead,
its edges reflecting
the glaring overcast.
Here's what the Indians left
he says, and as they cross
to the hilly woods beyond,
he tells her of all the people
who lived here on the land
before it was theirs.

She suddenly sees time change
from a daily now
to a long yesterday
with rivers and rocks,
people and clay and trees
walking the years,
and turning the arrow around
so it points the other way,
she gets her first glimpse
of all the tomorrows
just as wild geese shadow above,
calling across the sky.

Noon

Noon of a winter bare,
flat platter of white sky
serving up a sameness,

hanging time
like a drooping wash
drawn out pulley-slow,

and she plods a path
of endless chores
from broom to barn to bread,

work so familiar
she toils without thought
her body, so worn,
joins hands with numbness,

and she watches
the dim hot stone of sun
hiding behind
a fraught face of clouds,

and already sees tomorrow—
dim moon, dull sun—
still another noon
torn from another day
trudging across
her
despairing
bones.

Trillium

Little Brother sat on the porch steps
watching plump brown towhees
hop and hide and nibble in Mama's garden.
Somehow this April afternoon—
the sun so bright in a wide blue sky—
had the boy kind of itchy,
like he wanted to fly or leap over trees
or dive into a cold, deep pond.
The dark outline of cedars up on the hill
looked thick with adventure;
surely new butterflies and newts,
even morels hid there in the woods.
And he fancied he could find
just the right kind of surprise
for Mama's birthday
to make her smile
that special way she did—
shiny as the sun on the river.

Problem was,
he'd never been up there alone before,
always Sister, sometimes Papa.
Asking permission
meant someone would tag along –
no surprise in that!
After all, six is old enough
to take a little walk up a hill.
If he sciddadled round past the back field
and cut up onto the road,
he'd get to the top,
see something right off,

and be back in a jiffy
before Mama even knew he'd left.
The boy high-tailed it
right off the porch and did just that.

As he plodded up the hill,
the sun warmed his dark shirt,
and sharp scents of pine lured him on.
A bee rushed past his ear
on its way to spring's sweetness,
and above him, crows circled,
crying warnings from the woods.
Thin sticks of bracken,
thorns of blackberries pulling at his pant legs
set him more determined to reach the top,
and he pushed through salal and swordfern
thickening the border of trees.

He stepped into the woods with a sudden shiver.
In the sudden cool shadows,
huge trees sheathed in moss stood over him
like fur-lined animals.
Stringy green hair hung down
from long, reaching branches,
and he could hear clicks and snaps
from the underbrush.
Around his feet wild ivy twisted
as if to trap him in their thin, grasping fingers.
He took a deep breath,
then whistled to feel brave,
before plunging on.

It seemed he struggled through the woods
for a long time
before coming smack up to a giant cedar.
It was like a wall,
and he touched it...nose to trunk
to stretch his arms for measuring.
Layers of thick bark folded and creased
like pages of an old book, and
ants and blue-green beetles traveled up and
down its seams.

Here was another world
of plateaus and valleys and crevasses,

with spider webs crossing over a slash of bark
like silvered rope bridges;
and powdered, light green lichen
sprinkled the bark's edges
like soft green grass.
Above him,
a robin suddenly trilled a long melody,
singing his last bit of fear away.

Through the tall legs of trees descending
downwards,
the lowering sun shot a beacon of soft yellow,
drawing him further.
As he ventured down towards it,
he tried to be careful
not to step on twigs and deadfall
that would crack and snap,
breaking the quiet—
maybe he might catch the sight of an elk or
stag, even a fawn...
too dark, or maybe too late, for butterflies.

He bent, brushing thorny vines and leaves away,
looking for tell-tale wiggles and bumps of morels
under some of the conifers,
but found nothing.

The drop grew steep
and, slipping and grabbing part of thin twigs
of brush, he slid, landing in damp, soft earth.
Sky opened from the ceiling of trees,
allowing the sun to pierce the darkness
like a long spotlight
onto a ravine covered in clover.
In the center were hundreds of stars!

He stepped gently into the clover
and picked a star.
Three white petals glowed
on a stem of three wide green leaves—trillium!
This is what he would bring back for Mama.

With one hand full of plucked trillium, he
climbed out of the ravine,
slogging through brush and snaggles of vine
as the sun began to send gold and pink streaks
to the clouds bunching up above him.

He ploughed on,
hurrying at the thought of night,
and when he finally crested the hill
looking down at the farm,
a crescent moon came sneaking out
from thick dark clouds.
The farm windows were lit,
and he could see Mama
standing on the porch
looking out into the night.

He rushed to her
and thrust the closed and crushed trilliums
into his mother's open arms.
Happy Birthday, Mama.
I picked these just for you.
Mama just held him tighter and tighter,
and he didn't see the tears
on her smiling face.

Fiddle

Of an evening
cool and crisp as an autumn apple,
Grandpa took up his fiddle
and stepped out on the porch.
His gnarled fingers grasped the bow,
and slow at first, to his smooth caress
the fiddle began to sing a rising song
soon coming long and quick and jumping,
so his knees bent and his foot slid round,
and he kicked, brisk and bouncy.
And his shoulders swayed as he played,
leaning to the fleet, winding beat,
lurching forward—back
like riding his rocking chair—
until it wasn't Grandpa there
but a young man, raw-boned and nimble,
he and the fiddle simply one,
stirring up his story:

Years at sea with swollen hands and frozen cheeks
seeking blood and guts of yet one more whale;
years on boats with crabbing pots lost in churning tides,
mind numb in the knowing a river's hungry toll;
years in woods with ax and fire clearing a place a stay—
a way to plow and seed, fill the need to root and grow.

and the fiddle wailed and cried all time's passing
the fiddle sobbed and sighed for dreams unlasting
then laughed and took flight,
dancing up the sky,
two-stepping stars,
calling out to the far side hill
just as the red harvest moon
rose to trip across the tips of pine.

Wheelbarrow

It was of an August morn
and Grandma set her hat on,
the one with wisps of cornflowers
blue as her smiling eyes,
and gathered up her garden gloves,
ratty and torn,
her favorites, worn
through many a planting year.
Yesterday she had canned the cherries,
and baked Grandpa's chosen pie,
with marionberries,
and today she was just plain eager
to get out and dig.
She almost did a jig,
quick-stepping to the garden
bursting with spinach and greens,
carrots and sweet peas,
which she always strung up
like her own spider web
for catching their pink and lavender
butterfly buds.

But first to the shed for the wheelbarrow.
Each year its wooden wheels
wobbled more, and wooden sides
clearly showed it was more cart than barrel.
Rickety and wriggling when moved,
mighty cumbersome and heavy
to lift and shove,
it was the only source of contention
between Grandpa,
and Grandma's intention
to do it all by herself.
So there she went,
staggering and weaving,
wheelbarrow held tight
despite
the splinters already piercing her hand
from jagged wooden handles,
while Grandpa sputtered, heaving
himself out of his rocker
to stomp down the garden path
and once more make his stand.

Heavens knows the whole family
was ready for their innocent tiff,
if two young deer hadn't just then
crossed the road,
wandered as easy as you please
up to her blooming sweet peas
to nibble in delight bud and leaf.
It would have been a sight,
but the deer made the difference.

Wheelbarrow thrown aside,
Grandpa and Grandma both
fixed on shoo-ing and clapping,
and the deer kept munching
and trip-trapping
their delicate legs
like a genteel dance,
as if it were their right,
invited as guests, not to beg
or sneak, but to prance and eat
to their heart's content.
Papa and Sister and even Auntie
laughed to beat the band
but Mama came to the rescue,
carrying out the dishwater pan
and splashing both deer in the face,
so their huge dark eyes startled,
and out of the garden they flew,
leaping back into the wood,
which, as Grandma said,
was their proper place.

And there the wheelbarrow
lay shucked,
the wheel finally off
in the ruckus,
wood sides scattered
like discarded rail ties,
chipped handles soap-spattered—
it had met its sad demise.
Grandpa scowled,
then growled,
Good riddance!

Snow

Morning opened hail-sprinkled, white as sugar
on the surface of winter rhododendrons and
blooming heather, and the crunch and slip of
her tenuous steps in night's leftover storm drew
a cautioned track across the crinkled garden.
The cold wind breathed easier as if finally relieved
from a long climb, and she stood there by
the bare crab apple tree, the quiet embracing her,
with only a far-off hound dog heard close-up.

It was then the clouds ruffled and softened
like a large white mother hen settling in,
and the snow feathered out, first descending
small and splotchy, then circled around,
tossed and juggled on the back porch and
out to the hemlocks where it thickened
and took a direction, sweeping up the hill
over to the spruce woods, layering in
a silence along the ridge, only boot tracks
darkening the sheet of white along the road.

And she swept back to years before, Mama
there under the white blanket of that long
coughing gasping winter when snow outside
lit the room mute and cold with a dark-dotted
track of blood on the turned-down hem of
bed-sheet, and when she held Mama's head up
to ease the choking, the white chenille coverlet
burst blood-red roses, spreading steady
like blotting red ink til Mama stopped trying.

Time got hollowed out after that, not one tear or sorry,
just worry about how to bury Mama
in the frozen ground, and what to do with Papa
locking himself up in the back room, shouting out
the window into deaf snow, raging at black ravens
out in black trees as if it were all their fault.
Five days he wouldn't eat, then his terrible silence
finally broken by one piercing crack of rifle.

And she came to know Alone—
a long while her world dimmed,
more silent than the snow.

Neighbors Over Ninety

She's making apple pie; he's dozing a bit,
little kittens run across the old linoleum floor.
Clutter and comfort warm the room,
and soon she tells her tale.

~

Her mother in law was one of the original families and
at eighty years old gave ten acres of dairy land along
the slough to her son.

Theirs was the land of grass and fence
and one red barn—
so they moved into it,
milkroom as kitchen, granary as bedroom,
and set up a pump and barrel
to get water from the nearby falls.
They started building the house
using timber from the nearby mill,
hauling parts of an abandoned home
crouched on the other side of the pasture.

Then was the time of autumn rain and quiet sun and
the old apple orchards waiting long years,
Gravenstein and Elstar and Earligold
even Arkansas Black
all longed for the picking.
She itched to sink her fingers in dough
hear her husband's contented sighs
over sweet blackberry wine and pie—
but first a decent house!

Starting with one cow, a flock of fryer chickens, seeds
of cucumber, tomato, pepper and lettuce,
she dreamed of sweet peas and marigolds and rooms of
laughing children.
He logged for a living, she crossed the bay to stand the
day with other women—
Chinese and Finn and Swede—
in the cannery on the river.

And life before this dimmed almost to dream—
Her mother dead when she turned seven
Papa, swearing there was no God, no heaven,
gave her away to good-intending folk
—and kept the boys.

With no Mama's voice, no Mama's hand
her days were lonely shadows
enclosed in high ceiling and dark walls,
doors shut in smothering protection
thick as summertime wool blankets
and one simple regulation:
no playing no crying,
til she upped and left—
out the door without a thank you or good-by,
just walked ten miles back to Papa.

Earned her keep in his boarding house,
watched over brothers,
worked wash tub and kitchen.
Schooled in sewing, ironing,
and when not to speak,
she held her own when she had to
and was known as her mother's daughter
by the old townfolk

It was the blue dress with the white lace collar
stitched by her grandmother long dead
that she wore the picnic day she met her husband.
The dress just called out to me, he said.
that and her eyes, deep as Norwegian midnight.
Out of Oslo at thirteen, he sailed six years at sea
til that morning in Vladivostok
when his heart cried *Enough.*
and coming across the Pacific once again,
jumped ship in Portland,
with a hunger for earth and cows and trees.

He made his way west to the River's mouth,
just in time for that Sunday outing
where he found Summer under the big maple,
a girl sitting so fine and fair
like she'd been waiting there, wearing a blue dress
and smiling all his tomorrows.

~

She turns to the old man next to her
nodding and chuckling at their story.
How 'bout some apple pie?

NORTHWEST
Rainforest Pioneers

Windstorm

The wind announced its arrival
by whipping and slashing
hemlocks up on the hill
as they stood like resolute martyrs.
It surged down, flinging gulls and crows
into sliced-open barn doors,
and slamming down the potting shed.
It tore out the wood-staked fence
so tediously placed by Papa in last summer's heat,
herding confused, wide-eyed cows towards the estuary,
and ravaged Mama's garden
before settling on the invasion of the farm house.

The wind came uninvited,
thrusting door in, window out,
spilling into bedrooms like a swarm of bees
impelled to cluster and scatter,
rushing to flood into hair and ears and throats.
It burst into kitchen and parlor,
screaming a hunger,
shaking and ripping drapes and shutters
like a starving dog on the loose.

And Mama flung her body over Little Brother
pressing him, smothering him
there on the carpet floor—mother-fierce,
while Papa's leather chair rolled forward
then back past tipped lamps and skidding wardrobe,
and Grandpa gripped the closet doorknob
in a futile attempt to hide from the wind's grasp,
as Sister was tossed like a sock doll against the wall.

The wind roared an anger savage
as if this family were to blame
for its long lonely journey
from arctic ice, down craggy coasts
to the tormented riverway.
And all about was clamor and howl,
a rampage resounding
in a thundering shower of wail.
So that when it suddenly stopped,
all of them crawled out, mute and amazed.
The wind, exhausted, had died,
leaving the living—and silence hung in the trees.

Claudia Harper

Seining

The sky is apricot, fuzzy
with splinters of light covering still water
as the boy stands in his uncle's small boat
slowly approaching the islands
that appear and disappear with the tides,
their mounds of sand netted by long grasses
caught in the dawn light
like thin iridescent fish.

Centered on one island await horses,
Clydsdales and Pecherons
watching the incoming boats,
their muscles tingle
in the coolness of morning,
rippled energy matches a shimmering river.

The boy remains in the boat
while Uncle and other fishermen—
small boats spread over the channel—
wade into the river
to ride wagons in the ebb tide.
Horses thresh fish from water
harvesting night's catch
from strong nets set on the outbound tide
wide across the waterway
between the sand islands.

The boy can't see the submerged wagon.
He only sees Uncle, holding reins,
vanish underwater, along with Uncle's legs,
half of his uncle seems to float
along the river's surface.
He only sees half a horse chest-high
plunging against the river's might.

As the horses pull up onto the sand bar, water
drips and glistens,
foams around their shaggy hoofs
like the silvered salmon
thrusting and sliding over each other
in a mounting thickness of heavy seines.

All along the stretch of sand,
the boy sees a line of bending fishermen,
bulging arms pulling in unison wide nets,

the boy sees a line of straining horses
pulling in unison wide nets,
the boy sees a wriggling mass of salmon
using their last bit of strength
to fight for their last river's breath
before being hauled into the waiting boats.

The yellow morning sun drawing light across forests
beyond the channel
seems to also draw the changing tide in—
the power of the ocean joining the power of the river—
for the boy sees the sandbar begin to shrink,
compressing the grassy islands,
pressing the fishermen to unhitch horses,
to corral the horses
until the next ebb tide.

The boy gazes back at the receding islands
as his uncle's boat turns for home.
He wonders at the horses, the men,
the river, the fish, the seines
and begins to know what strength is.

Beach

The January day broke open blue and cloudless
as rare for winter as the sound of robins,
and Mama was all a-dither
filling lunch baskets with pear pie and salmon cakes,
apple wine and fresh-baked bread,
for the boy's papa had announced
opportunity knocks but once and it was now or never
so best take the horses and cart and travel a far road
to the spit of sand and a rolling ocean—
if they all wanted to get to the beach!

With the cart fairly brimming with excitement,
heavy with the likes of the whole family—
what with Uncle and Grandpa and Sister
and Mama, wearing her favorite cherry-rimmed hat;
and all sorts of blankets and jugs and shovels and buckets,
even an accordion and banjo and fiddle enclosed in a smalltrunk—
the horses galloped pell-mell
alongside the slough and muddy stream.
It took a dayful to wind the road,
sometimes muddy and sometimes planked,
passing spruce woods and boggy pastures
to a barge waiting to ferry them across a murky creek.
And then they edged a huge river glaring in the winter sun,
wide as the ocean, smooth as Mama's looking glass,
and Papa said *still waters run deep.*

The horses trotted on, coming first to a small harbor of boats,
where the air was raw fish and slapping nets,
and next plunging into a dark, piney forest
between two hog-backs,
only to pull up onto a rise of sand dunes
where a welcoming noon sun hung in the wide sky
warming the crest of shimmering beach.

Such a wonder of white sand sinking bare feet,
such a wonder of sea blue and green and gray
with white beards of foam flowing on each curved wave!
The men hurried to build a fire
while the boy scurried down, then back,
racing ripples of rolling water and stone.
Then, standing alone,
he spotted a solitary tern winging low between sky and sea
as if searching which way to go,
and he suddenly felt very small and drifting.

It was the call of rising music, a tuning-up strings
that drew him back to his place of belonging.
Lying down, the heat of sand
pressing through his back,
winter sun still smiling a blessing,
he watched Grandpa begin to circle the fire,
fiddling a round of bouncing sound
in time to his steps.
Papa followed, his accordion smoothing the path
towards Uncle's banjo, hopping and tripping notes
like skipped stones across water.

Mama stood up, then taking Sister's hand,
they bowed and circled and do-se-doed
skirts shifting and rustling over the sand,
hats slipping and hair coming loose
with naught but a shrug from Mama.
And fire and waves struck percussion—
fire crackling a red fast beat
waves hitting sand with a roar and hiss—
so the boy, caught in the rhythm,
clapped and hooted, whistled and called.

And the sky rolled white, as clouds stepped in
as if to join their dancing
and the wind rose up, sand pricked the air
but still they went on dancing.

And he suddenly saw the circle
of fire and sky and wind
of sea and bird and family—
all one turning dance.

He heard the chord
floating up like drifting sparks
joining the vast, graying sky—
all one harmonious song.
And he declared,
This is the happiest day of my life